Forgiveness

52 SHORT REFLECTIONS FROM *I FORGIVE YOU, BUT...*

Forgiveness

LOURDES E. MORALES-GUDMUNDSSON

Pacific Press® Publishing Association
Nampa, Idaho
Oshawa, Ontario, Canada
www.pacificpress.com

Designed by Steve Lanto
Cover design resources from iStockPhoto.com

Additional copies of this book may be obtained
by calling toll-free 1-800-765-6955
or online at http://www.adventistbookcenter.com

ISBN 13: 978-0-8163-2244-2
ISBN 10: 0-8163-2244-9

07 08 09 10 11 • 5 4 3 2 1

A Word to the Reader

Forgiveness sounds so easy, so desirable—until someone hurts us deeply and we come face-to-face with the need to forgive. Then we discover how difficult—how incredibly difficult—it really is to forgive someone who has wronged us.

Grounded in Scripture, *I Forgive You, But . . .* by Lourdes Morales-Gudmundsson, leads us through the human dimensions of forgiveness from the viewpoint of those who have struggled with it, prayed about it, and searched God's Word for what He has to say about it. As the Bible makes clear, forgiveness is a two-way street: We must forgive others who have wronged us, but we must also accept forgiveness, for we have wronged others—and God. And both

directions—forgiving and being forgiven—are vital to our peace of mind and our relationships with God and with each other.

I Forgive You, But . . . is a mini-manual for peace. Through forgiveness, we can find inner peace in the midst of turmoil. When Jesus promised us His peace, He contrasted it with the short-lived peace the world offers: " 'Peace I leave with you; my peace I give you. I do not give to you as the world gives. Do not let your hearts be troubled, and do not be afraid' " (John 14:27, NIV).

All of us have forgiveness issues that we need to address. An increasing amount of research has focused on the idea that forgiveness is actually physically healing as well as spiritually healing. Could this be why God emphasizes the importance of forgiveness? Could this be why He promises so repeatedly to forgive us our sins if we only ask Him to? Could this be why He is so insistent that we forgive others? Because He knows forgiveness is the path to peace and healing and wholeness—physically, mentally, and spiritually?

Forgiveness is so easy to talk about, yet so hard to live! In her book, Lourdes Morales-Gudmundsson unfolds the process of for-

giving and being forgiven. The book you are holding contains 52 short reflections on forgiveness—each composed of a quotation from *I Forgive You, But . . .* paired with an appropriate Bible text. Although it may not take you long to read them, these reflections will provide you much to think about. The 52 little readings about forgiveness in this book can help you experience that peace that Jesus has promised—the peace that passes all understanding (see Philippians 4:7).

And if you find these reflections helpful, and you'd like to read *I Forgive You, But . . .* in its entirety, look for information on the last page of this book.

—The Publisher

1

*B*ring your petitions, and return to the Lord. Say to him, "Forgive all our sins and graciously receive us, so that we may offer you the sacrifice of praise" (HOSEA 14:2, NLT).

Peace comes when we *really* believe that God through Christ has forgiven us and continues to be willing to forgive us when we confess our mistakes and weaknesses to Him and to each other.—p. 18.

*I*f we confess our sins, He is faithful and just to forgive us our sins and to cleanse us from all unrighteousness (1 JOHN 1:9).

The mandate of forgiveness is so central to our faith, that to ignore it is to ignore our very salvation.—p. 21.

*I*f you forgive men their trespasses, your heavenly Father will also forgive you. But if you do not forgive men their trespasses, neither will your Father forgive your trespasses" (MATTHEW 6:14, 15).

We are never more miserable than when we withhold forgiveness and never happier than when we give it.—p. 22.

*I*n this is love, not that we loved God, but that He loved us and sent His Son to be the propitiation for our sins. Beloved, if God so loved us, we also ought to love one another

(1 JOHN 4:10, 11).

*W*hen an injustice stops the flow of love,
we seek the way back to love over the bridge
of forgiveness.—p. 22.

*L*ove one another; as I have loved you. . . .
By this all will know that you are My
disciples, if you have love for one another"

(JOHN 13:34, 35).

We may not get a plaque for forgiving a negligent parent or a faithless spouse, but, in the long run, it is that quiet, intimate decision to release wrongdoers from what should rightfully come to them that will  identify us as true sons or daughters of God.—p. 22.

6

*Y*ou shall love the LORD your God with all your heart, with all your soul, and with all your mind.' This is the first and greatest commandment. And the second is like it: 'You shall love your neighbor as yourself' "

(MATTHEW 22:37–39).

18

$\mathcal{L}$ove is every bit as powerful in the human psyche as is hate. No matter how awful the sin perpetrated against us, we are still capable of forgiving because we are still capable of loving.—p. 33.

$\mathcal{T}$herefore I say to you, her sins,
which are many, are forgiven,
for she loved much. But to
whom little is forgiven, the same
loves little" (Luke 7:47).

We can still forgive, because we, the injured ones, are the ones who will be most blessed by doing so.—p. 33.

8

Peter came to Him and said, "Lord, how often shall my brother sin against me, and I forgive him? Up to seven times?" Jesus said to him, "I do not say to you, up to seven times, but up to seventy times seven"

(MATTHEW 18:21, 22).

Forgiveness is not simply a one-time event, but an ongoing process.—p. 36.

Finally, all of you, live in harmony with one another; be sympathetic, love as brothers, be compassionate and humble. Do not repay evil with evil or insult with insult, but with blessing, because to this you were called (1 Peter 3:8, 9, NIV).

A basic tenet of forgiveness [is that]: We
have to let go of something in order to
receive a greater gain.—p. 39.

10

$\mathcal{Y}$ou, being dead in your trespasses and the uncircumcision of your flesh, He [God] has made alive together with Him [Jesus], having forgiven you all trespasses (Colossians 2:13).

*F*orgiveness calls on the highest moral
powers given to us by God
and is central to everything we are
and do as Christians.—p. 40.

11

They [Joseph's brothers] sent messengers to Joseph, saying, "Before your father died he commanded, saying, 'Thus you shall say to Joseph: "I beg you, please forgive the trespass of your brothers and their sin; for they did evil to you." ' Now, please, forgive the trespass of the servants of the God of your father." And Joseph wept when they spoke to him (GENESIS 50:16, 17).

28

*F*orgiveness is motivated by love and our capacity to be generous.—p. 43.

12

I will forgive their iniquity, and their sin I will remember no more" (JEREMIAH 31:34).

*F*orgiving an "enemy" is what the Old Testament God does constantly. His tirades against the children of Israel were immediately followed by promises of forgiveness and restoration, if only they would honor God's law of love. But even if they didn't, He was willing to take the risk of giving them yet another chance.—p. 49.

*T*he commandments . . . are summed up in this one rule: "Love your neighbor as yourself." Love does no harm to its neighbor. Therefore love is the fulfillment of the law

(ROMANS 13:9, 10, NIV).

Love, manifested through a forgiving spirit,
is the fulfillment of the law.—p. 51.

14

*W*hat a difference between our sin and God's generous gift of forgiveness. For this one man, Adam, brought death to many through his sin. But this other man, Jesus Christ, brought forgiveness to many through God's bountiful gift (ROMANS 5:15, NLT).

$\mathcal{T}$hrough His [Jesus'] overarching act of pure forgiveness, we all were set free from condemnation. . . . We did nothing to earn it—no acknowledgments of sin, no repentance or confession. It was His love, His empathy, His compassion, His infinity of spirit that gave us [the] . . . forgiveness [that] restores us to eternal life.—p. 51.

15

*H*e who covers his sins will not prosper,
But whoever confesses and forsakes
them will have mercy (PROVERBS 28:13).

*H*uman forgiveness is, on the one hand, that gratuitous act of grace that asks for nothing and opens the way for healing, and, on the other, it is that act of grace that *does* require transactions of confession and change so that the forgiveness promise can be kept.—p. 53.

16

*Y*ou are a forgiving God, gracious and compassionate, slow to anger and abounding in love" (Nehemiah 9:17, NIV).

*F*orgiveness lies at the very core of what it means to be a Christian, and, within Christianity, the Christian God was the first to exercise this virtue: " 'God so loved the world that he gave his one and only Son, that whoever believes in him should not perish but have everlasting life' " (John 3:16).—p. 56.

17

*Y*ou have heard that it was said, 'An eye for an eye and a tooth for a tooth.' But I tell you not to resist an evil person. But whoever slaps you on your right cheek, turn the other to him also. If anyone wants to sue you and take away your tunic, let him have your cloak also" (Matthew 5:38–40).

*I*t is one thing to love; it is quite another to keep loving in the face of injustice, cruelty, and rejection. That is why to talk about love without also talking about forgiveness leaves love crippled.—p. 56.

18

The LORD passed before him
[Moses], and proclaimed,
"The LORD, the LORD, a God merciful
and gracious, slow to anger,
and abounding in steadfast love
and faithfulness, . . .
forgiving iniquity and transgression and sin,
yet by no means clearing the guilty"

(EXODUS 34:6, 7, NRSV).

*I*t is precisely His [God's] eagerness to forgive that requires Him to discipline His wayward children. Just as God cannot keep loving if He cannot discipline or set limits, so we cannot keep loving if we don't set boundaries through the process of forgiveness.—p. 56.

*B*e kind to one another, tenderhearted, forgiving one another, just as God in Christ forgave you (EPHESIANS 4:32, NKJV).

*T*hese are the royal antecedents of forgiveness for the Christian believer: God, the Eternal Father, through the Son of God and Man, the Messiah, gave His life to forgive us, and He forgave us so that we might forgive one another.—p. 57.

20

The God of all grace, who called you to his eternal glory in Christ, after you have suffered a little while, will himself restore you and make you strong, firm and steadfast (1 PETER 5:10, NIV).

*I*t is helpful to consider the sufferings of others to place one's own suffering in perspective, thus opening the way to forgiveness.—p. 58.

21

*F*orgive, and you shall be forgiven.
Give, and it will be given to you: good
measure, pressed down, shaken together,
and running over" (Luke 6:37, 38).

*F*or a Christian, the answer to Why forgive at all? can simply be, Because the Bible tells me to. And it tells me to because forgiveness is good for me and because I can trust the Author of the Bible to want what's best for me. Forgiveness is present where the divine intersects with the human in the daily struggles of human life. If it can help me live a healthier, happier life, why not forgive?—p. 59.

22

*Y*ou, Lord, are good
and ready to forgive,
And abundant in mercy to all those
who call upon You (PSALM 86:5).

*W*hat sets the Christian religion apart from any other world religion is the centrality of forgiveness in its theology and liturgy.—p. 59.

23

*I*f anyone is in Christ, he is a new creation; the old has gone, the new has come! All this is from God, who reconciled us to himself through Christ and gave us the ministry of reconciliation: that God was reconciling the world to himself in Christ, not counting men's sins against them (2 CORINTHIANS 5:17–19, NIV).

Our ability and willingness to forgive has everything to do with whether or not we have allowed God to re-create us. It also has to do with whether or not our forgiveness is going to have staying power.—pp. 60, 61.

24

*I*f you bring your gift to the altar, and there remember that your brother has something against you, leave your gift there before the altar, and go your way. First be reconciled to your brother, and then come and offer your gift" (Matthew 5:23, 24).

*W*e are made new in Him [God] through His forgiveness of our sins, but now we must share the forgiveness that we received so graciously. Yes, we must help other sinners be reconciled with God, but we must also be reconciled with those whom we have offended or who have offended us.—p. 61.

25

I say to you, love your enemies, bless those who curse you, do good to those who hate you, and pray for those who spitefully use you and persecute you, that you may be sons of your Father in heaven" (MATTHEW 5:44, 45).

What makes Christians different from non-Christians is their capacity to love and forgive and intercede, even for those who are their declared enemies.—p. 62.

26

*J*udge not, and you shall not be judged. Condemn not, and you shall not be condemned. Forgive, and you will be forgiven" (Luke 6:37).

Repeatedly, throughout the New Testament, the motivation for forgiveness is the fact that we have been forgiven. If God was willing to sacrifice His only Son to forgive you and me, the least He can expect from us is that we make a minimal sacrifice to forgive an erring brother or sister.—p. 63.

27

I will greatly rejoice in the LORD,
My soul shall be joyful in my God;
For He has clothed me with the
garments of salvation, He has
covered me with the robe of
righteousness, As a bridegroom
decks himself with ornaments,
And as a bride adorns herself
with her jewels (ISAIAH 61:10).

If I do not love and value myself as God values me, I will not be able to love my neighbor. Similarly, if I do not forgive myself as God has forgiven me, I will not be able to forgive my neighbor. Accepting God's forgiveness is accepting His love for me—I have to accept both in order to share either.—pp. 63, 64.

28

I acknowledged my sin to You,
And my iniquity I have not hidden.
I said, "I will confess my transgressions
to the Lord," And You forgave the iniquity
of my sin (Psalm 32:5).

Living the life of goodness is living a life of forgiveness.—p. 64.

29

*T*herefore, as the elect of God, holy and beloved, put on tender mercies, kindness, humbleness of mind, meekness, longsuffering; bearing with one another, and forgiving one another, if anyone has a complaint against another; even as Christ forgave you, so you also must do (COLOSSIANS 3:12, 13).

Because we have been forgiven, we are morally obligated to pass on the favor we have so generously received from God.—p. 68.

30

*W*hich is easier, to say, 'Your sins are forgiven you,' or to say, 'Arise and walk'? But that you may know that the Son of Man has power on earth to forgive sins"—then He said to the paralytic, "Arise, take up your bed, and go to your house" (MATTHEW 9:5, 6).

*J*esus . . . equates forgiveness with healing. For Him, there was no difference. He seems to recognize that a guilty conscience or an angry heart can create a sick body, and that to truly heal a sick body, one must address the damaged conscience.—p. 88.

31

*H*ave mercy upon me, O God,

According to Your lovingkindness;

According to the multitude of Your tender

mercies, Blot out my transgressions.

Wash me thoroughly from my iniquity,

And cleanse me from my sin.

For I acknowledge my transgressions,

And my sin is always before me

(PSALM 51:1–3).

*O*ne of the hardest people to forgive is *you*!

. . .

Self-condemnation is the cruelest of tribunals and one that has the potential to last a lifetime.—p. 95.

32

*T*herefore I say to you, whatsoever things you ask when you pray, believe that you receive them, and you will have them. And whenever you stand praying, if you have anything against anyone, forgive him, that your Father in heaven may also forgive you your trespasses" (MARK 11:24, 25).

*P*rayer is one of the
least-understood
resources for the
Christian life in general
and for Christian
forgiveness specifically.
—p. 96.

*W*e do not present our supplications
before You because of our righteous deeds,
but because of Your great mercies.
O Lord, hear! O Lord, forgive!
O Lord, listen and act! Do not delay
for Your own sake,
my God" (DANIEL 9:18, 19).

$\mathcal{Y}$our bad behavior is irrelevant to God's willingness to forgive. It's your repentance and confession that matter to Him. It's hard for us to imagine just how ready and willing our loving Father is to forgive us if we only ask.—p. 97.

34

*B*lessed is he whose transgression is forgiven, Whose sin is covered. Blessed is the man to whom the LORD does not impute iniquity (PSALM 32:1, 2).

*A*ny way we decide to begin our forgiveness journey, the destination is one and the same—forgiveness that restores the flow of love in one's life.—p. 104.

35

*T*herefore let us not judge one another anymore, but rather resolve this, not to put a stumbling block or a cause to fall in our brother's way (ROMANS 14:13).

One of the most helpful tools to move us toward forgiveness and keep us on the forgiveness road is empathy. Empathy is that human capacity to make room in the self for the pain of another, to feel what they feel.—p. 108.

36

*H*ave mercy on me, O God,
according to your unfailing love;
according to your great compassion blot
out my transgressions. Wash away all my
iniquity and cleanse me from my sin. . . .

Restore to me the joy of your
salvation and grant me a
willing spirit, to sustain me

(PSALM 51:1, 2, 12, NIV).

If our confession to the wronged person and to God is sincere and our lives demonstrate the necessary changes, God has forgiven us, even if the person we wronged hasn't. With God's forgiveness we have all we need to forgive ourselves and to move on.—p. 118.

37

*L*ove suffers long and is kind; love does not envy; love does not parade itself, is not puffed up; does not behave rudely, does not seek its own, is not provoked, thinks no evil; does not rejoice in iniquity, but rejoices in the truth; bears all things, believes all things, hopes all things, endures all things. Love never fails (1 CORINTHIANS 13:4–8).

*M*aking forgiveness permanent is looking at the ex-offender with different eyes. We may recognize the same behavior, but now we understand where it comes from because we've gently restored the person in our own mind.—p. 127.

38

When they had come to the place called Calvary, there they crucified Him, and the criminals, one on the right hand and the other on the left. Then Jesus said, "Father, forgive them, for they do not know what they do" (LUKE 23:33, 34).

*E*ven as He gasped for His last breath, Christ was beyond the touch of His enemies because He had already forgiven them.—p. 128.

39

Moses returned to the LORD and said, "Oh, these people have sinned a great sin, and have made for themselves a god of gold! Yet now, if You will forgive their sin—but if not, I pray, blot me out of Your book which You have written"

(EXODUS 32:31, 32).

*A*nyone who has experienced forgiveness knows that forgiving calls on the highest moral powers given to the human race.—p. 130.

40

*B*rethren, if a man is overtaken in a trespass, you who are spiritual restore such a one in a spirit of gentleness, considering yourself lest you also be tempted.

Bear one another's burdens, and so fulfill the law of Christ (GALATIANS 6:1, 2).

*F*orgiveness is just that: a choice. And it is a choice we are always free to make, no matter how difficult the circumstances. It can be made in the face of calls for revenge, retribution, restitution, or fairness—there'll always seem to be some "rational" motivation not to forgive. But we are wired by God to forgive and live.—p. 130.

41

*R*emember not the sins of my youth
and my rebellious ways;
according to your love remember me,
for you are good, O LORD. . . .
For the sake of your name, O LORD,
forgive my iniquity, though it
is great (PSALM 25:7, 11, NIV).

Forgiveness is not aimed at righting the wrong or changing the past. It is meant to release the victim from the *negative effects* of the wrong, all the while acknowledging the latter's awfulness.—p. 130.

42

*I*f your brother sins against you, rebuke him; and if he repents, forgive him. And if he sins against you seven times in a day, and seven times in a day returns to you, saying, 'I repent,' you shall forgive him" (LUKE 17:3, 4).

*I*s there such a thing as forgiving too much? That question can be answered with a categorical No! Forgiveness as we understand it here is a state of mind in which we consciously choose to release our offender from our anger and expectations of justice, wishing him no ill, only good. And we can never do too much of that!—p. 131.

43

You do not desire sacrifice, or else I would give it; You do not delight in burnt offering. The sacrifices of God are a broken spirit,  A broken and a contrite heart— These, O God, You will not despise (PSALM 51:16, 17).

*N*o life sentence, no form of revenge, nothing but forgiveness can bring peace in the face of a great injustice. This is so because injustices are not just legal offenses; they are emotional experiences that affect the mind and the body.—p. 137.

44

Speak comfort to Jerusalem, and cry out
to her, That her warfare is ended,
That her iniquity is pardoned;
For she has received from the
LORD's hand Double
for all her sins" (ISAIAH 40:2).

*F*ar from approving a wrong, forgiveness . . . stops and looks carefully at the wrong done, allows the emotions that the wrong elicited to have expression (tears, anger, etc.), and then seeks restitution through some process of justice.—p. 137.

45

$\mathcal{L}$et the wicked forsake his way, And the unrighteous man his thoughts; Let him return to the LORD, And He will have mercy on him; And to our God, For He will abundantly pardon (ISAIAH 55:7).

*I*saiah teaches that forgiveness must be transactional, not because God needs any acknowledgements of sin, but because human acknowledgement of sin is central to human salvation.—p. 141.

46

*I*f we say that we have no sin, we deceive
ourselves, and the truth is not in us. . . .
We make Him a liar, and His word
is not in us (1 JOHN 1:8–10).

*T*rue forgiveness has to do with accountability; false forgiveness has to do with selfish self-preservation. True forgiveness serves the other; false forgiveness serves the self. True forgiveness empowers both the victim and the offender while false forgiveness disempowers both.—p. 142.

47

*W*e also rejoice in our sufferings,
because we know that suffering produces
perseverance; perseverance, character;
and character, hope. And hope does not
disappoint us, because God has poured out
his love into our hearts
by the Holy Spirit

(ROMANS 5:3–5, NIV).

*F*orgiveness not only has the power to make suffering bearable, it also has the power to suffuse suffering with meaning.—p. 145.

48

*J*udgment without mercy will be shown to anyone who has not been merciful. Mercy triumphs over judgment! (JAMES 2:13, NIV).

*D*aily contact with the source of moral and spiritual strength is what will help us as mature Christians to have the victory over the selfishness and hard-heartedness that prevents us from moving beyond our demands for justice to true forgiveness and fullness of joy.—p. 148.

49

*I*f My people who are called by My name will humble themselves, and pray and see My face, and turn from their wicked ways, then I will hear from heaven, and will forgive their sin and heal their land" (2 CHRONICLES 7:14).

Prayer will make our decision to forgive endure. It is not humanly possible . . . to face the daily challenges of the forgiveness promise over the long run without divine intervention.—p. 152.

50

*B*less those who persecute you; bless and do not curse. Rejoice with those who rejoice, and weep with those who weep. Be of the same mind toward one another. . . . Repay no one evil for evil (ROMANS 12:14–17).

*D*aily placing the forgiven one in the
hands of the Almighty will go far
in releasing us from the load of carrying
that person in our hearts and minds
in destructive ways.—p. 152.

51

*O*ne thing I do, forgetting those things which are behind and reaching forward to those things which are ahead, I press toward the goal for the prize of the upward call of God in Christ Jesus (PHILIPPIANS 3:13, 14).

*W*e honor God when we allow Him to overcome our inner enemies of pride and fear and anger for us. We honor Him when, through His power and not our own, those inner victories move us along the forgiveness road to ultimate triumph.—p. 158.

52

*W*hen we were overwhelmed by sins,
you forgave our transgressions (PSALM 65:3, NIV).

*W*hen, through the workings of prayer, we place our trust in God and let Him sit on the thrones of our minds and hearts, we will find that our decision to forgive was the right one and that we are safe in the hands of Him who never tires of forgiving us.—pp. 159, 160.

I forgive you, but...

We *know* we should.
Why is it so *hard?*

Lourdes E. Morales-Gudmundsson, Ph.D.

Of course, I've forgiven him, but . . .

𝒴ou find yourself mentioning the offense to a friend, remembering how the incident made you feel, and how it affected your life. Afterward you feel guilty. Why? Because Christians are to forgive and forget, right?

This book is for Christians who believe that forgiveness is important to their spiritual journey but who may not understand what forgiveness really is. It's for those who just can't seem to move on from a deep hurt.

Paperback, ISBN 10: 0-8163-2201-5. US$13.99.